Desert Storm: Dreadnought

By

Joseph B. George

ISBN: 1-4140-2421-5 (e-book)
ISBN: 1-4140-2422-3 (Paperback)

This book is printed on acid free paper.

1st Books - rev. 11/24/03

Desert Storm: Dreadnought

Combat is a life-changing event that affects the human spirit tremendously. Soldiers enter combat not knowing that their lives will be changed forever. Before the first bullet is ever shot, the soldier's mind is numb and he is prepared to give his life for his country.

After I graduated from high school, I did my basic training at Ft. Knox, Kentucky which is the home of Armor. That is where I was introduced to modern warfare. I certainly did not know what I was in for, but I was young and extremely cocky. The first thing I learned was not to even *think* about not following orders. Then I was pushed mentally and physically further than I could ever imagine. High school football was a joke compared to basic training.

The culture shock began when I stepped off the bus at Ft. Knox, Kentucky. We ran off the bus to screaming drill sergeants, ordering us to form lines. Drill sergeant Conyers was over 6 feet tall and all muscle. I tried to run away from him, but he called me back to his platoon. They told us that we would never forget our drill sergeants and they were right. It was drill sergeants Kay and Conyers' job to transform us into soldiers, and they did a tremendous job.

We were different from anyone else at Ft. Knox because we were tankers, the backbone of the U.S. Army. We trained harder and longer than everyone else. The tank is the most superior and feared weapon on the battlefield when it comes to ground warfare. The first time I saw a M1A1 Abrams

tank I was overwhelmed. It was 60 tons of
steel and had a top speed of 50 mph. I was
18 when I graduated from basic training and
I was in the best shape of my life.

Furthermore, I was stationed at Ft.
Riley, Kansas, with the 1st Infantry
Division, also known as the Big Red One. My
first day at work my unit was in the field
and they placed me on the commander's tank.
That is where I learned that the average
tank battle lasts 15 minutes. I also
learned how to fight the Soviet Union. This
training would prove to be vital during
Desert Storm.

The first time I pulled battalion
duty, I realized how much tradition the Big
Red One has. I slept in a room with
spectacular pictures of the division in
Vietnam. It was simply amazing. They were
valiant soldiers and had hearts like
gladiators. It put me in the frame of mind
to fight to the death with everything I
had. I was making the transition to

becoming a killing machine. I was starting to understand where the nickname "No Mission too Difficult, No Sacrifice too Great, Duty First" came from. However, it was 1990 and I didn't think a war would break out in 2 years. Little did I know that I was about to be placed on the front lines of the battlefield with the most destructive fire power the world had ever seen.

M1 Tankers spend an enormous amount of time in the field training for battle. It was 65 degrees below zero with the wind chill factor, and we had to train as if it were 70 degrees. If you took your gloves off for longer than 10 seconds, you would be frost-bitten and your flesh could stick to the steel. My tank was my home. All I could do at night under those conditions was tap my feet on the floor to keep my circulation going. I was assigned to Delta Company 2nd Battalion, 34th Armor and we were Top Guns. Our motto was "Dreadnought."

Every month we would simulate fighting the Soviet Union in the field. Once a year we went to the National Training Center in California to simulate fighting the Soviet Union for 30 days. That is where I learned the seriousness of combat. For example, if my tank was disabled, we would still fight it sitting still.

Meanwhile, In August 1990, we were at the gunnery range at Fort Riley when we learned that Iraq had invaded Kuwait. Immediately rumors were spreading like wildfire that we were going. Unlike the National Training Center in California, we lived in the barracks for two weeks and we had access to television. Secretary of State Dick Cheney flew in, escorted by Black Hawk helicopters to check the status of our readiness. While the tanks were firing on the range, he was nervously jumping around, shaking his head "yes." He asked me how old I was and why I joined the Army. I told him I joined to pay for college. He was extremely intelligent. Furthermore, he took some pictures with my tank crew and left. After we returned from the gunnery range, we started making preparations to deploy to the Gulf, even though we had not received orders. Finally, while watching CNN on our lunch break, we learned that we were going.

First of all, the first objective was to get the tanks painted. It did not take long at all to get this done. However, we did spend long hours in the night doing it but we knew how important it was that everything was done right. Next was the dangerous job of driving the tanks on the trains. It was done without any injuries. It was an awesome sight, to see all those Heavys lined up, waiting for action. It gave us a sense of invincibility. The tanks were railed to a port in Beaumont, Texas. From there the division's equipment was shipped to Saudi Arabia.

I made my will and gave my mother power of attorney. My company commander told us that he was not authorizing us to go home for the holidays but he was not telling us not to go. We knew not to miss the flight to Saudi Arabia. Meanwhile, my company was going to be the first tanks to clear the Iraqi mine fields. Everyone knew that a tank battle lasted 15 minutes and it was clear that we would not leave the mine fields alive.

At this point, we still did not know the exact date we were leaving and it was almost Christmas Eve. I was 19 and none of my family members had ever missed a Christmas; I was not about to start now. I talked to my buddy from Louisiana and he felt the same way. He said he would never miss a Christmas if he was in the United States. We knew we were not coming home from the war and it was Christmas. Three of us drove to the airport in a blizzard. It

was so cold in Kansas that the gas was
frozen in the pump.

I went home for Christmas, thinking
this could be my last time seeing my family
and friends. I had the best friends in the
world. My family was great and it was
Christmas. Christmas Day, my mother sent my
cousin to find me because I hung out all
night. I took some family photos and said
my last goodbyes. On the way to the
airport, I told my mother to make one last
stop at my best friend's house. When I
walked in, his family was eating Christmas
dinner at the table and tears were rolling
down my face. His dad was a Vietnam Veteran
with a purple heart and he immediately
stood up. My best friend told me that I was
coming back, but he did not know what I
knew.

Finally, I was at the airport and I
hugged my family for the last time. I saw a
guy in my company at the airport in
Charlotte that was not supposed to be

there. He had dark sunglasses on and we hardly said anything to each other because of the situation at hand. He had a look on his face of a man that had seen his family for the last time. It was as if he had the world on his shoulders. He knew it was all over and he was preparing mentally to fight this war. We had too much on our minds to sit together on the plane. The situation was becoming tremendously intense.

Everyone that went home returned safely. During physical training, the captain asked me how my trip was. I told him it was great. He did not ask me if I went home, but it seemed like he knew. Those are the kind of guys that you want to go to war with. The orders came down that we would leave on New Year's Eve. Some soldiers were breaking down mentally. The pressure of combat was taking its toll and we were forced to keep each other together. In war, you are only as good as the guy beside you. It was like a bad dream. The reality was, we were not coming back. I was only 19 and I was in a no-win situation. We could not drink any alcohol within 48 hours of departing.

The barracks were so quiet on New Year's Eve that you could hear a pin drop. I kept checking my duffle bag over and over again to make sure I had all of my equipment. I saw a gunner from South Carolina lying on his bed, watching everything that passed by his room. He was terrified. He could not believe that we were not coming back. Everything that we trained for was about to be tested. We knew we had to clear the mine field and open the breach in Iraq at all costs. That was the only job given to us, because we would not make it out alive. One thing was for sure: it would be short and devastating. I played the scenarios in my head to prepare myself for destruction and certain death. It did not matter what anyone said or thought.

This was the ultimate sacrifice, and it was no joke.

At this point, I had crossed the line of no return. It was all about doing my job the best I could. I had no intentions of losing or surrendering. It was all or nothing. I made up in my mind that I would do everything I possibly could to make it back home alive, but I was at peace with death. On the 21-hour flight to Saudi Arabia, my friend from Louisiana showed me some card tricks. We stopped in Belgium to refuel.

We arrived in Saudi Arabia on New Year's Day, 1991. We lived in tents until we moved out closer to Iraq. About two weeks later, our ship arrived while we were playing tag football in the desert. The ship was escorted by Apache attack helicopters. It was the first time I had seen an Apache in person, and it was an awesome sight to see. We stopped playing football to take in the moment. Play time was over and it was time to get down to business. Our tanks were unloaded and inspected. We were not supposed to use those tanks, because we had new ones waiting for us in Germany from when we fought the Soviet Union - brand new tanks that were more sophisticated, and which had more firepower, were issued to us. The National Guard received our old tanks.

Some marines came over to look at our tanks and they were amazed at the firepower. A tank consisted of a .50-caliber machine gun, an M-16 rifle, a grenade launcher, two 240 machine guns, and a 120mm cannon. My personal weapon was a 9mm. The Marines knew they did not have anything on the ground that could match it, and they were amazed. However, I got a chance to see the Apaches up close. They were awesome. There is no other attack helicopter in the world that can match it. A tank is helpless if attacked by an Apache, and it crossed my mind many times.

Trucks called hets moved our 60-ton
tanks closer to Iraq. Saudi buses
transported us to our tanks. Rumors were
circulating that the king of Saudi Arabia
offered each American soldier $9,000 if the
U.S. sent women home and $6,000 if they did
not. The U.S. said that we were not
mercenaries. Meanwhile, we stayed at one
location and moved out frequently. Life is
very uncomfortable, living on a tank. When
I had to use the bathroom I walked about 50
yards from the tank and dug a hole.

One day I was standing on top of my
tank and an A-10 thunderbolt was coming
directly towards me. I was helpless and I
thought I was going to die. I was so scared
that I shit in my pants. It's big, bulky
and its main job is to destroy tanks. I
later found out that the Vietnam Veterans
call it "Puff the Magic Dragon." The reason
a tank battle is short is because there is
so much firepower on the battlefield.

Most of the time was spent waiting for the war to start in the desert. That was very unusual, because we worked most of the time. That gave us more time to think about the situation. However, we did test our weapons systems in the desert. The 120mm cannon packed a tremendous punch. That's when I found out that the rounds were made out of depleted uranium. I also knew that nuclear submarines were ready to launch a nuclear attack if needed. Rumors swirled that if the war got out of hand, the Arab nations would fight with Iraq. For some reason I was not worried about a chemical attack, even though the threat was definitely there.

I daydreamed most of the time about going to college and raising a family. I was switched to the executive officer's tank with the guy that was in the airport in Charlotte. The gunner was from New York, the driver was from Georgia, the commander was from Ohio, and I was from North

Carolina. We got along and worked well together. However, the pressure was mounting as the deadline to leave Kuwait drew closer. I was 19 and I had never seen a grown man scared. People were being pulled off tanks and people were trying anything to get out of the war. My mind was set on the task at hand. We knew we were going to fight, and Saddam promised a bloody fight. We were up to the challenge.

While sitting around waiting, an armored Iraqi vehicle rolled into our location. It did not last long before someone destroyed it. Nothing was ever said about the incident, because we knew what awaited us. The Iraqis had time to build a trench filled with mines and chemicals. That is why it was predicted that the first tanks through would not survive. Although we were in a no-win situation, our morale remained high. We were going to fight to death, using every trick we knew. We had plenty of firepower, so we were confident.

We also had something to come back
for. Even though they said we were not
coming back, it would not be because we did
not give the effort. The last stop before
combat was the Saudi-Iraqi border. Iraqi
soldiers tried to cross the border at night
and we picked them off with machine guns.
Our night vision capabilities were amazing.

The air war started and Operation
Desert Shield was now Operation Desert
Storm. We listened to the news on the
British Broadcasting Channel with our
walkman radios. The Allied Forces' air
power did a tremendous job. It was not long
before I could see the burning flames over
Baghdad. The sky was orange at night
because of the bombing raids. We waited
anxiously as the B-52 bombers dropped their
massive bombs. Sometimes the ground would
shake after a B-52 strike.

It was an awesome sight, to see B-52s
escorted by fighters. We controlled the
sky, and it was a comforting feeling. The

air campaign dominated the Iraqi military; no stone was left unturned. The United States bombed Iraq 24 hours a day, and the results were demoralizing. During the weeks of the air war, I had time to think about every situation that I was going to face. It was the first time that I was not busy since I joined the Army.

After a month of intense bombing, it was time for the ground war to begin. War cannot be won by airpower alone, and the tank is the king of the battlefield. The captain gave the orders that the ground war would start February 24, 1991. The original plan had not changed. Our objective was to clear the Iraqi mine field so the rest of the 7th Corp could pass through. We were going through Iraq while everyone else attacked Kuwait.

Everything had come down to this. It was truly the moment of truth. My entire unit was ready. We were prepared to fight until the bitter end. The word "surrender" was never mentioned at anytime. I felt like I had the firepower I needed to get the job done. When the Big Red One spread out and prepared for battle, I saw tanks for as far as my eyes could see. We had over 360 tanks. I did not realize we had that much firepower, even though we had four battalions of tanks. I saw a tank shoot another tank in the rear before the ground war started. The tank that was hit was getting ready to shoot back, but a cease-fire came over the radio. Again, no questions were asked, because we knew the situation at hand.

I was waiting for the Air force to bomb the mine field, but it never happened. A tank commander who was also an Army Ranger gave a message over the radio that revealed the intensity of the situation. The tone of his voice was incredibly strange. It was as if he were already dead. I don't know why the captain did not give that speech.

That night, the refueler told me that
I better get as much fuel as possible,
because he did not want to be anywhere near
a tank when the battle started. He was
terrified and I understood why. There's
nowhere to hide in the desert, and
everything is a target. We expected them to
use chemicals, so we put on our chemical
suits.

The captain gave one last briefing
that night before we attacked. We hardly
talked, because we were focusing on what we
had to do. There are a million things that
can go wrong in war, and you have to be
prepared. Nothing beats preparation. The
United States usually strikes at night,
because then we have the advantage. The
driver of my tank told me that his last
unit's motto is "hell on wheels, we strike
at night."

We began the ground assault at around
4:00 or 5:00 in the morning. There were two
green lights that we were supposed to pass

through that no one on my tank saw. All of a sudden, my tank crew was lost in total darkness. We kept asking the commander for help and all he said was keep going north. I had already seen the friendly fire incident, and I knew that the Iraqis were north. I did not know if I would be killed by friendly or enemy fire. At the same time, tanks were opening fire on anything that was out there.

I did not want to die like that. I tapped the gunner on the shoulder and signaled to him that I was going to kill the commander if he kept going north. He just turned around in his seat and continued to scan the area in his sights. My adrenaline was flowing to full capacity. This was not supposed to happen, and we had not planned for it. I had lost it, and I was awaiting death. I felt helpless and I was a sitting duck.

When dawn came, my tank was cutting across the massive formation of friendly

tanks with their gun tubes pointing
directly towards us. I was horrified, and I
could not comprehend how lucky I was to be
alive. We radioed the commander and linked
up with the company. A call came over the
radio that the Marines had been gassed and
we were going to Baghdad. The Marines were
fighting in Kuwait and we were in Iraq. I
knew in my heart that we did not have
enough troops to fight in Baghdad alone,
and I was terrified.

We met little resistance in breaching
the trench, and we were all astonished.
Most of the Iraqi soldiers were waving
white flags and surrendering. They were
terrified, tired, and hungry. We threw
boxes of ready-to-eat meals and water off
our tanks as we passed by, for them to eat.
It was the kindest act of humanity that I
have ever seen. At that time, we were all
human beings.

Unfortunately, the rest of the ground
war would not be as friendly. After we

breached the mine field and entered Iraq, there were dead Iraqi soldiers being eaten by dogs. We dismounted our tanks and stared at the soldiers' corpses. All I thought about was their families. There I was, 19 and getting a first-hand look at war and death. It was real and this was war. None of us understood it, whether we were 19 or 40. Nobody said a word. My mind and body was numb. War is something a person will never completely understand unless they experience it for themselves. My mind went from almost being killed to looking at dead bodies being eaten by dogs.

I was once again focusing on the next mission. I did not have time to think about what I had seen and done. At night fall, we stopped in a strange place in Iraq that had a lot of curves. There are not any landmarks in the desert, and we were in "no man's land." Anything could have happened there. It was almost like a maze. It was pitch black. A Vietnam Veteran said over

the radio that this was a good place for an
ambush. I said to myself, *if anyone comes
on this tank tonight, they're dead.* I
wondered how I was supposed to sleep. I
laid next to my m-240 machine gun with my
9mm pistol, and went to sleep. A tanker
knows everything that is going on around
him when he is sleep.

Our next mission was to stop the
Republican Guard from escaping. Everyone
knew that they were the elite, and once
again the length of a tank battle loomed in
our minds. It was as if we were facing
certain death – not because they were
better, but because there is so much
firepower on the battlefield and tanks lead
the way. There is nowhere to hide in the
desert and a tank is completely vulnerable
to air strikes.

We moved out in the morning and drove
all day. My head kept hitting the top of
the tank because I was exhausted. My body
literally shut down. We drove all day and

fought the Republican Guard that night. It was burning vehicles everywhere. It was like going towards the World Trade towers when they were falling, instead of fleeing. The driver of the tank was so tired, we almost collided with a burning vehicle. Shots were ringing out everywhere. Tracer rounds and explosions filled the sky. Occasionally, artillery would light up the sky with illumination rounds, so that we could see the entire battlefield. My adrenaline had taken over and the Republican Guard did not stand a chance.

You would have to see it to believe it. Heavy machine gun fire filled the night air. It was the Big Red One at its best. Every tank was hitting its target. We did not leave any survivors. We trained in extreme weather conditions and we confronted the Republican Guard with the best tank division the world had ever seen. Everyone was up to the challenge. It was a complete annihilation of the Republican

Guard. We proved to the world that we were unstoppable.

The Dreadnought battalion kept the history of the first Infantry Division intact. All the hard work and training paid off. When the cease-fire was announced, they celebrated because the war was over. The elation on the soldiers' faces was priceless.

You never know how much you love your family until you stare death in the face. It was as if our families were right there with us. I have never seen grown men so happy. They could not have been happier. However, I was not as happy. My mind was numb and I had been through hell. Some things happened to me prior to the ground war that made me bitter. I have never talked about it to this day, and I won't now. That is just the way it is. I sucked it up and I did my job. Soldiers learn to drive on.

The orders came down for us to provide
security for the generals so they could
complete the Iraqi surrender. I was
standing on the ground, talking to one of
my friends, and we heard a loud explosion.
I immediately ran to my tank, assuming that
war had broken out again, but it was
engineers destroying Iraqi weapons. Some
soldiers questioned the decision to end the
war so soon. They hoped that they would not
return. I knew I was getting out in
November, so it did not matter to me.

We drove through the burning oil
fields on the way back to Saudi Arabia.
Black smoke and flames was all that we
could see. It looked like hell. At noon it
was pitch black. I touched the tip of my
nose and smut was all over my finger. I
knew that could not be healthy, and I
wondered how it would affect me later.

Now that the war was over, the big
question was when we are leaving. I was
selected to make sure the tanks returned to

Saudi Arabia. The truck that carried my
tank kept breaking down. I was forced to
wait for a new truck in a location that I
was not familiar with. In other words, I
was lost. However, I went into the city and
met a young Arab boy in a store. He was
about 12 or 13 years old.

I called home and my uncle, who is a
Vietnam Veteran, answered the phone. I told
him that I did not know where I was and I
asked him how things were at home. He was
calm and told me things were fine. Little
did I know that my mother's closest sister
was dying of cancer. My mother told me
before the war that things would be
different when I returned.

Arab women came into the store to look
at me. They were dressed in black and wore
veils. Their bodies were covered, except
for their eyes. My Arab friend told me they
came to flirt with me. They were not
supposed to look me in the eyes, but some
did anyway. It was not often they were able

to see an American soldier in person, and I jumped at the chance to see their culture. Some Afghanistan soldiers came in with long beards and AK-47s. All I had was a 9mm. They were frowning at me but I was friendly towards them. I was 19 and fearless. I did not have any idea what kind of situation I was in. I would do anything to find life outside of war.

Furthermore, my Arab friend invited me to his house. I was not supposed to be in that city in the first place, and here I am going to someone's house. I was hesitant but I went. He had some friends there that spoke English fluently. They were mesmerized by me, and he had a deep love for American soldiers. He asked me questions like how violent was America and would I ever come back to visit. We sat around in a circle, talking and learning about each other's culture. They loved President Bush because he freed them from Saddam.

When it was time for me to leave, my friend was very sad. It was almost as if he was losing a family member. It made me feel good and I was proud to be an American soldier. I went back to my tank and moved out again. We came across an Arab man that was very friendly. He asked us if we had any guns, in case Saddam came back. We told him no, but we talked and he gave us gifts. We met a Bedouin in the desert and he invited us to dinner. Neither he nor his family spoke English, but we ate and communicated the best we could. It was a wonderful experience. It was another reminder that we were all human and we should act accordingly.

After about two weeks, I finally made it to Khobar Towers in Saudi Arabia where the rest of my company was. They were glad to see me and they were worried about me. They did not have any idea where I was and they had not heard from me. A Vietnam Veteran was anxious to see what I looked like. I was glad to be with my friends. It was the last stop before we went home. After all the killing and danger, I was finally about to go home. We were able to go to the mall and around town. However, during public executions we could not go in the city. About two weeks passed and we left Saudi Arabia. We arrived in Maine to welcome banners and American beer. It was an awesome feeling, but I still was not home yet.

Life after war is devastating and unpredictable. It is far worse than combat itself. I left Desert Storm a changed man, and everyone knew it but me. I was used to living with death, and it had made me numb. I could not walk down the street at night without thinking someone was trying to kill me.

When I was discharged from the Army at the age of 20, I did not know what I wanted to do with my life. All of my emotional energy was spent. Alcohol was the only way for me to cope with all the pain I felt inside. People feel like Desert Storm was a war that America won with few casualties. Unfortunately, there are thousands of American soldiers that are sick or already dead. Oil well fires, pb pills, shots, sand, insects, and chemicals are some causes for these sicknesses. It could be a combination of all of the above. We could have been exposed to low levels of chemicals that were destroyed during and after the war. One theory is that the wind blew low levels of chemicals on us from bombing raids and from when the engineers destroyed chemical weapons after the war. One thing is for sure, soldiers are complaining about symptoms ranging from chronic fatigue to muscle pain.

After the war, I was running with the battalion flag during physical training and I ran out of breath. One day I was playing a game of basketball with my cousins, I was breathing extremely hard and I was out of breath. I was 21 at the time and I knew that something was wrong, but I was in denial. Every summer I tried to build wind by jogging, but I just could not do it. I recently found out that other Desert Storm Veterans are having the same problems. Needless to say, I keep trying no matter how painful or depressing it is.

No one understands. Some of the medication that we used had not been tested. I can't walk up a flight of steps without sweating and breathing hard. If I do something as simple as spending time with my family all day, I'll be exhausted that night and the next day. I cannot bend down to tie my shoes because of back pain. My entire body aches at times, especially when I am working out. If I take medication for some of these symptoms, I feel like someone is beating me in the head with a baseball bat.

This is Gulf War Syndrome. No one wants to be sick. I named just a few symptoms, but there are many more. We are expected to live normal, productive lives when we re-enter society. No one tells us about post-traumatic stress disorder (PTSD) unless you have already done something bad. I did not know that it was normal not to want to be around people after I came back from combat. I went from walking away from fights as a teenager to wanting to kill someone. Everything I tried to do failed, and I had to live with that.

There were mornings when I could not get up to go to work because I was too tired. Alcohol made the fatigue worse. My first job after the war was as an aircraft refueler for a private company. I refueled private and commercial planes. One day I worked a double shift and by the end of the day I was making errors like forgetting to put the fuel caps on planes. My supervisor told me not to work a double shift anymore. I had no idea at the time that it was

because something was wrong with me,
because I was in denial.

I had to move back in with my parents
to get on my feet. Everyone in my family
was educated, except me. All three of my
sisters had graduated from college and were
living on their own. No one understood how
I could lay around the house for days and
not do anything. Before I was 16, I worked
in tobacco fields and bought my own school
clothes, even though my parents could have
bought them. I rode my bike over 15 miles
and over long bridges with my cousins to
the blueberry field to pick blueberries. It
did not pay a lot of money, but I was young
and I wanted my own money. I played soccer,
football, baseball, basketball, and the
saxophone. I had plenty of friends and I
loved to be around people. I was one of the
most outgoing guys you could find. All of a
sudden, the war is over and I am laying
around the house, not looking for a job and
I did not want to be around anyone.

Furthermore, things got worse when I
was convicted of two driving while impaired
(DWI) charges. I lost my driver's license
for four years. I was losing everything
that I had worked for in a short amount of
time. My life had taken a drastic turn for
the worst. People were talking about me
being different, but I did not care. I
found out quickly who my true friends were.
I did not have any control of my life, and
all I could think about was war. When I was
around my family and friends, I could not
sit down and talk to them, nor could I look
them in the eyes. I was always on edge, and
waiting for something to happen. I was
ashamed at the way my life was turning out.

It is hard for me to explain what
combat does to the human spirit; you either
kill or be killed. In between the actual
combat, there are a million ways to be
injured or killed. I did the very best I
could to live a normal productive life, but
nothing worked. I did not want to drink,

but I could not stop. My family was embarrassed at my behavior. I quit going to family reunions and I did not even go to my mother's retirement party. No one understands the pain I feel inside.

Now that I am older, I understand why people do not understand. Combat becomes a part of who you are. It is not something you can just put behind you, and you get on with your life. If people really understood combat, they would not think about disrespecting a veteran. All of the veterans that I talked to knew that the D.C. sniper was a veteran. I know veterans whose lives have been turned upside down. They would do anything for a normal life. It is a heavy price to pay to be a warrior. Every step you take on the battlefield could be your last.

After years of moving in and out of my parents' house, I was finally starting to give up. People often asked me if I was back home again, but I remained positive because I knew I would leave again. This time was different; I did not see a way out and I was tired of getting the same results. I had an older cousin with a house out in the country; it was the only place on earth that I went to where I did not have to worry about anything. My cousin and his brother accepted me for me. I could drink as much as I wanted and I was at total peace. It was so peaceful that I would drive three hours to go there at any time.

All of a sudden, one of the guys in the neighborhood started coming around. I did not go anywhere else in that neighborhood, because I was drinking and I did not want any trouble. Sometimes when I would be talking, I noticed this one particular guy would be looking at me like he hated my guts. I knew the guy did not like me, so I never said anything to him that would make him angry. He must have mistaken me for being weak. I told my friends that this guy was continuing to give me problems and that I did not want to hurt him. This guy was over 6 feet tall and I am a small guy. Keep in mind that I was frustrated at the way my life had turned out.

I was at the point where I did not have anything to lose. Finally, one night I was drunk and some words were said. This time I defended myself. He told me if I said anything else, he was going to drag my little ass all through the yard. I said to myself, you might drag me through this yard but it will not be tonight! I immediately started thinking about the war and being killed. I went into the house looking for something to defend myself with but my cousins talked me out of it. I kept thinking about what he told me and I hit him in the head with a bottle. My cousins that were there lied and said I hit him for no reason. I had to walk around town with people looking at me like I was crazy. It was terrible, but it happened. I do not know what would have happened to me if he had not dropped the charges.

I ended up getting another DWI the night before I had to go to court. I thought about taking the police officer's gun and running out of the station. Instead, I went home and my mother had already known about the situation. Later, my dad had me arrested for taking his car without permission. It was the same officer that arrested me for DWI. He asked me did I remember him, but I was too drunk to recognize him. The guy that I assaulted did not press charges against me, and neither did my dad. My family made me go to a substance abuse center for veterans and it was the best thing that could have happened to me.

I dreaded the fact that I had to get help. To me, it was a sign of weakness. I was at my lowest point. Things could not have been any worse for me at that time. My

life was down the tubes. My mother and my
Aunt Kathy drove me to the veteran's
hospital in Salisbury, North Carolina. We
spent the night in a cozy hotel because
Salisbury is about five hours from New
Bern. The next morning, we drove to the
hospital where I would be spending the next
30 days. The admissions officer was a
veteran that did two tours in Vietnam. The
veteran that was being admitted before me
stated that he had hepatitis a and b. I was
shocked, because you could not tell
anything was wrong with him. I said goodbye
to my family, not knowing that my life
would change forever.

The first thing that I noticed was
that all of the veterans took a lot of
pills. The first thing I did was see the
doctor, and I left his office with a brown
bag full of medicine. I could not believe
it, because I was still in denial. I was
walking down the hall with my pills,
wondering what was happening to me.

Everyone, including the staff, was staring at me because I was so young. I was 28 at the time. One of the nurses walked up to me in the cafeteria and asked me how old I was. They all knew if I was there then something was terribly wrong.

The first two days were rough. I felt like I made the wrong decision. However, I started making friends and my outlook changed. One of my friends was a truck driver with a cocaine problem. He killed some people in an accident and he had trouble sleeping at night. His attitude was terrible and people did not like being around him. He told me that since I was there, the only places left for me to go were prison or the graveyard. He told me if I was there, my life was over and I was in big trouble. Then he told me to look at the sign outside; the sign said "Mental Ward, 4th Floor." I knew if I kept doing what I was doing, that was my next stop.

I was at the breaking point of my
life. I made up my mind then that I would
never drink again. The truck driver was not
a Vietnam Veteran, but he was in the Army
during that time. That was his 15th trip to
rehab. He opened my eyes up to the road I
was on, and I really appreciate him for
that. However, I learned how to play chess
while I was in jail and it gave me
something to do. Chess gave me a chance to
learn how to live without drinking. My
cousin Boo, who is like the brother I never
had, inspired me to learn the game. It also
gave me the opportunity to break away from
my friend because his attitude was so bad.

I have always had a tremendous amount
of respect for Vietnam Veterans. I had
never heard any war stories from one but I
was about to get my chance. My Uncle Wink
is a Vietnam Veteran and I have always
admired how he kept his life together. A
guy named Walter moved into my four-man
room and he was a Vietnam Veteran. The next

day in group therapy, the counselor asked
him why he was there. He told her it might
be to help someone else. Walt was an
airborne sniper in Vietnam and he had been
to several treatment centers. One of the
first questions I asked was, "When does the
nightmare end?" The Vietnam Veterans told
me it does not end.

These were not counselors that learned
something from a book. These were the men
that fought and saw their buddies killed,
and lived to talk about it. I was listening
and it has not gone away for me. For nine
years, I was all alone. No one understood
how I felt - not even my mother, and she
understands everything. It was all coming
together now. I found a new family in
Salisbury. I found out why I felt like
that, and it was normal. I had been around
all types of people in my life, but these
men were different. They had problems on
top of problems. Add alcohol and drugs to
PTSD, and you have some real problems. One

veteran told me he took 14 pills every day.
Another said he was tired of it all and
thought about suicide. Late one evening,
the guy with hepatitis a and b played and
sang the most beautiful song I have ever
heard on his guitar, about being homeless
and Jesus. Just because we were homeless
did not mean that Jesus did not love us,
too. We all had major problems and we were
looking for help. I was closer to God there
than I have ever been in my life. During
the day, we went to classes on subjects
ranging from what stress and drugs do to
the body, to learning how to stay clean and
sober.

One night, the Vietnam Veterans had a
discussion about the war in my room. It was
very intense. They were sharing poems that
they wrote during the war. The poems
revealed how afraid they were and how badly
they wanted to go home. Later that night,
one of the veterans kept pacing back and
forth through the room. I tried to calm him

down in my sleep. In other words, I was
sleep-talking.

I understood why they do not talk
about the details of the war. Walt told me
I was sleep-walking one night and he told
me everything I did. I remembered doing
some things like going to the bathroom, but
I did not remember everything. When we were
getting ready for bed that night he opened
the curtains so he could see everything.
(Veterans are trained to be aware of
everything that is going on.) I asked him
to tell me some stories about the war and
he did. He said he was ordered to go down
and inspect a tunnel and found three dead
American soldiers with their penises cut
off and stuck in their mouths. One of the
guys was talking about "Puff the Magic
Dragon" saving him in one of his poems. One
of the lines went something like, "Puff the
Magic Dragon, please get us out of here."
The sadness and seriousness of the tone of
his voice still remains fresh in my mind.

One year later, I asked my Uncle Wink what Puff the Magic Dragon was, and he told me it was an A-10 warthog. That is the same plane that made me shit in my pants during Desert Storm. I had asked my uncle once before did he know what I did when an A-10 came directly at me, and he said, "You shit on yourself." I was shocked. He had to have been in a similar situation to know what happened, but I never asked. The A-10 has so much firepower, I did not know it was around then. You do not want to be in the same area with one if you are a tanker.

It was all starting to come together. Some questions I had were finally being answered. Group therapy was held once a day. The counselors focused on one person daily and helped him to solve his problems. That is when I realized how wrong a person can be when judging someone you do not know. Several people in my group had cancer, and I did not know it. It was easy for me to listen to their problems and come up with my own solutions. However, when it was my turn, it was not as easy as I thought it would be. My counselor started asking me questions that I did not like, and I became extremely angry. I got out of my seat and started walking around.

The next day at group therapy, nobody wanted to sit beside me. Never back a veteran into a corner. From that point on, the people in my group had more respect for me. The more time I spent there, the more I started thinking about the direction that my life was going in. It was becoming clearer that I was not alone in my struggle. I learned to stay away from parties and my old friends. Anything that could cause me to relapse was considered a trigger, and I had to stay away at all costs. I learned valuable lessons there that I still apply today.

Now that I was back home, I had to learn how to live sober again. It was like starting from scratch. Changing my friends was the hardest part of the process. I was used to living on the edge my entire adult life. Luckily, one of my best friends was changing his life also, and we made the transition together. I realized that I had to find something to take the place of drinking, so I played chess as much as I could. However, everything was different. My mind was changing drastically, and I was starting to see things clearer.

At the same time, I did not have any means of coping with the war. In that respect, I was alone again. I was fighting two major battles: addiction and combat. I began searching for answers to my problems, because that was the only chance I had to live a productive life. Unfortunately, there are not any solutions to my problems. That is the price you pay for being a warrior. Often people commit suicide or homicide after returning from war. Others live a life of drugs and alcohol. I hope this book will put combat in its proper perspective. There is no such thing as an easy war. Millions of soldiers' lives are destroyed forever.

Operation Iraqi Freedom put me right back in Desert storm. It was almost unbearable. I could not believe it. I knew that the only reason the war had not started earlier was because the equipment was not in place yet. It takes months to get the equipment in position for battle. I used to joke about watching the next war on television. When the deadline passed for Saddam to leave Iraq, I watched the news, waiting for the intense air raid. Instead, it was extremely calm. I told my friend that the war had probably already started.

The United States knows how to use the element of surprise. Desert Storm was the perfect battle plan for desert warfare, so I thought it would be used again. The air raid did not weaken the spirits of the Iraqi people, and it gave them hope to fight. In Desert Storm, we used B-52 bombers escorted by fighters to devastate our opponent. The Iraqi prisoners of war would lay face-down when an aircraft passed by. The power was turned off immediately, and we hit every target that enabled them to wage war. The world saw our firepower and that is why the Afghan soldiers ran when we invaded Afghanistan. They fought the Soviet Union for 10 years, but they knew they were no match for us, because of Desert Storm.

However, the ground war started too fast. There were not enough ground forces to fight that kind of war. I was devastated when I found out that the ground war had started, because I knew there were not enough troops. I felt like I was right there with them, fighting. My mind and my spirit were with them. Then I realized that the reason the ground war started so soon was because they had to secure the oil fields. The plan was to have more ground troops to invade through Turkey, but Turkey would not agree. The ground troops fought a tremendous fight. All I could think about was how lucky I was to be alive. I realized why it was so hard for me to get past the war, and why I had changed so much. I had nothing to be ashamed of.

I understand now why my family does not understand the way I feel. You have to experience it for yourself, to get the proper understanding. Grown men were terrified and did things to get out of going to war. I did my job to the best of my ability, and I put my life on the line. It changed my outlook on life and I made some terrible decisions. I learned not to take anything for granted and swore to live my life to the fullest for as long as I could.

America is a great place to live. You can be anything you choose to be here. This kind of freedom is not cheap. It comes with a heavy price that a warrior has to pay. I wish I would have known what to expect after the war was over.

I hope this book will help someone understand what a warrior goes through when the shooting stops. I would encourage anyone who knows a veteran who is having a tough time readjusting, to explain to him what is going on and get him some help. I did not have a clue that what I was going through was normal for combat veterans. My parents stood by me, even though my life was a living hell. My mother accepted and encouraged me, despite my situation. It would not have been possible for me to have made it through this without the help of God and his son Jesus Christ; I give Them all the praise and the glory.

About the Author

He finished his basic training at Ft. Knox Ky. in 1989. He served 2 years in the Army with The Big Red One. He also served on the front lines of Desert Storm in a M-1A1 Abrams tank. He is currently working on a BA. Degree in Social Work.